Amulet

Amulet

by Carl Rakosi

New Directions

ACKNOWLEDGMENTS

The poems in this volume written prior to 1939, in somewhat different form usually, made their appearance first in exciting little magazines of that day: *The Exile, Transition, The Little Review, Hound and Horn, Contact, Pagany, Palms, The New Act, Windsor Quarterly, Westminster Magazine, Lion and Crown, Two Worlds Quarterly.* Some also appeared in *Poetry, The Nation, The Objectivists Anthology, The American Caravan, Modern Things, Poetry Out of Wisconsin,* and in a booklet by Modern Editions Press. In 1941 James Laughlin published a selection in the *Poets of the Year* series entitled *Selected Poems.*

Recently *The Paris Review* reprinted "The Founding of New Hampshire" and "The Lobster." I hope this means that the second generation finds those years a good vintage.

I did not write again until April 1965. Some of this new work has appeared in *Poetry, The Massachusetts Review,* and *The Quarterly Review of Literature.*

To the editors, my thanks!   C. R.

New Directions Books are published for James Laughlin
by New Directions Publishing Corporation,
333 Sixth Avenue, New York 10014.

First Printing

Contents

To Andrew Crozier, who wrote the letter
which started me writing again,
And to my family.
L'hayim! Each of them came along just in time.

The Poem

comes in
like an ocean
blow
into my head

and goes out
as a small model
into the world,
smelling
like a rose,
        hm?

Dedication

to the house
and its white linen,

to the chub, his guts out,
the grass from his throat
and fresh herbs in his belly,

to the draper's English
whose sincerity is like a horse
and rider on a sanded path,

to Izaak Walton's English
sounding like the small bell
of the knife-grinder,

to the trout carved in the table
of the little fishing house
which gives greenwood to the water.

Good tongue to you all
who like the chub
are tied with splinters.

Grace Note

Since the world
has been my tuning fork,
I must have struck
a note myself
from time to time
which pays my debt
with honest affection,
undivided between
head and spring.

Good Morning

A yellow feather
of a note,

delighted bounding
canary birdcry!

Up, my Norwich,
spit the bitter

gravel out,
throw out the little

ball in midair,
grasp the cuttlebone

with male claws.
Come, my Coppy,

3

eat your seed.
The sun lights up

the lettuce leaf
between the bars!

Amulet

You are ideal,
o figurette,
and cool as camphor.
Your eyes are set
in small blue jadework
and your head stings
like a drop of witchhazel.

Bless the white throat
of this lady
drinking clabber milk
at a buffet lunch.

The Classics

The girls
wear earrings

on the water,
silver beaten

4

with a punch,
the carved end

striking out
two flowers.

This day
the young

men, sternum
in the water,

swim below
the cutter races.

Women used to
pass into

the public buildings
with a blue jug

on their heads
and stand

like statues
with the noses

knocked off,
commemorating

the signing
of the peace.

Woman

steps out
from a lily

into the clear,
bearing a quince,

creator
calling

the ships out,
radiant

in cloth
and water

like a daisy
in the hand.

She lifts
her skirt

and speaks.
The ships

are radiant.
Man rises

from the kiss
and answers Yes.

The Gnat

A greeting to Louis Zukofsky

Winter and wind,
the whole age

is an afternoon
around the house

a little snow
a sea blizzard

a yard clover
a lucky house

anabasis
for edelweiss

six rivers
and six wenches

the twelve
victories.

The Creator

Fresh mollusk morning
puts a foot out
from its bivalve
on the sea.

7

And in a moment
the underwater
fairy palm blooms

and all the trout
and mussel
come to life

and wrasse and sturgeon
dart through the water
with their hungry heads.

What have I brought home
in the skin of the sea cucumber
that look like wheels and anchors
under the microscope?

Pike-Eater's Song

The hours
come
into the city,

horses breathing
on a sprig
and fishermen

with ale glass
in a window
singing *Old Rose.*

The Clarinet

runs up
a water-
ladder quicker
than the soul
past gravity.

A temperate sun
inhabits its wood,
once green
and shady.

This small-
bored Ariel
a pipe
with elegant air-
holes to the mellow
lining of abstraction
has a gentle reed
on which I suck
and like to dream.

Man at Work

"Every other man
runs a business.
Every fourth man
is professional."

What in hell
is this?

It is a table
not with four legs
but with statistical legs.

This is that strangest
of all worlds, *numbers,*
which no one can enter
as a whole man
nor leave behind

for it is the very principle
of the mind at work,
its style, its strict proportions,
its alignment, its very faculty,

that timeless order
which is bilk to poets,
wholly without heart or humor,
immaterial as fairy,
yet the very frame of industry.

This is the grub of scholars
and the final
sawdust of the absolute.

Time to Kill

A man and his dog.

What fun
chasing twigs
into the water!

Young girls bicycle by
in pairs and plaid shorts.

A wind so soft,
one's whole
back tingles
with cilia.

A gentle lake.

The sun boils
at the center,
radiates the zone
for man
          and lays
a healing pad
across his nape.

An airplane small and flat
as a paper model
roars behind
the Virgilian scene.

An old man
tips his straw hat
down to shade
          his eyes,
pulls up his fishline
and moves on
to a new spot.

The poor small
wood louse
crawls along
the bark ridge
for his life.

11

Institutions

This way the little banjo
music enters the hotel.

This way the channeled ceiling
luminaires
            of the National
Bank of Commerce,
metal-finish crystal ground floor
and small grilled windows
and banking hours.

Lamp

with goddess,
        ivory-carved
Japanese lady,
        hands crossed
over breast, holding
        on her head
electric bulbs
        and batik
lamp shade.

Family Likeness

Above the fireplace
the portrait of an old man
with a fowling piece
and period whiskers,
Sir William Cavendish,
6th Bart., and brevet major,
11th Hussars.

Crest and shield:
a demi-man
affronté in armor,
the helmet adorned
with three feathers,
holding in the dexter
hand a scimitar.
Two miner's picks.
Omne Solum Forti Patria.

Needlework

Over the fan-tan table
and the tea and noodles
one admires the return
          to Lisbon
of the navigator on the needlework
who sailed the Hansa routes with linen,
point-lace, hardware, and camphor wood,
bearing private letters
from the Augsburg bankers,
the owners of the ships of Ghent.

13

Now with his own slave and a clock,
he stands under one sail,
                    looking home.
Before him coral, geese, boats,
and an unknown woman
                    under a palm tree
with strawberries charmingly
                    out of proportion.

The City (1925)

1.

Under this Luxemburg of heaven,
upright capstan,
                    small eagles . . . .
is the port of N. Y. . . . .

gilders, stampers, pen makers, goldbeaters,

fear of thunder
        speed
    the whore
        indifference
    son
        glioma
    water.

Tammany, McCoy,
the bronze doors of the Guaranty Trust,
the copper spandrels.

Orangerie and game room
with Old English tall twisted
stem engraved goblets
and Royal Copenhagen porcelain.

A mutton fat jade
Chien Lung
                    bowl
a toilet bottle
                    amethyst
stopper & a monogram shield.

A technical display.
You bought a perfume bottle
and a Chinese shawl.
Susannah set a headstone in St. Paul.

I'm inside waiting for a surprise.
I'm in love with the girl on the Wabash.
I'm alone with a hand in my hand
and a pair of wonderful eyes.

But I'm blue
I have to speak
I want to do
I want to see
the sights obscure me
the facts secure me.

The *Maine* sails out to sea.
The undertaker drives to Hartford.
Yesterday the ducks flew in a mackerel sky.
I had the allotropes of vision,
something historical at the controls
of North America,
heavyweight and metaphorical.

What are the facts?
They swept the city hall today,
they set the lathe dogs,
trimmed the tool posts,
scraped the bearings,
shellacked the knots.
They set the capital
upon the shaft.

Somebody has to drive the spikes,
pitch the gears,
oil the cams,
somebody has to kill the whisky.
Somebody has to speak.
What are the facts?

2.

Inland is
the goat in open field.
The milk is marketed.
Attend our table.

The sand
          and fluorspar
and the soda ash
make a blue
          aventurine glass
for this city,
          a lion rampant
on his hind feet, royally
clawing, tail whipped up.

16

3.

come, great city,
give us that old-time vaudeville:

"During the water movement
of the French horns
and the lovelace of a violin,
a wire from my girl. She says
'I love you but I need a deposit.'
Even the ventriloquist's dummy laughed
after we combed his pretty red hair
and set him on his tricycle."

Do you know the story of Sal?
She was a lonely little gal
with the lovelight in her eyes
and Mr. H.H. at the ivories.
And she was happy (honest to God).

In the season of Romain effects
and synthetic American lights,
she drove into a California suburb
in a high-compression gull-line Suiza,
rolling her Klieg eyes
like revolving doors.

Whereupon the jackass
full of animal gas
floated blissfully
into the dance
of the seven veils,
yakking: I have that
funny feeling again,
it must be love.

Commentary: nothing
so marks the copulative man
as a corkscrew and a bottle opener.

Question: Could you stand an old man
to a cup of coffee?
It's hard walking
with this silver plate in my head.

Come, great city,
                    you have full powers
of attorney to protect your friends.

4.

Immigrants from Warsaw
move into a furnished room
close to the stores,
under St. Chrysostom's carillon,
with a porcelain pitcher
and bath and hand towels
on the bed rails.

A new sign appears
in the ground-floor window:
Smocking, Hemstitching, Rhinestone Setting.

One hour from here
                    a loggia
above the pepper trees,
a tiny cascade and vines
above the bath house,
men and women driving
on the fairway, laughing,

surrounded by Galloway
pottery, garden furniture,
and white daisies.

5.

When the light sprang from the sea, blowing,
the window sintered and blew like Venus,
revealing my tenderness
                    and many minds
the way a night shot
discovers a beast drinking,
                    and my responsibilities
eating me as dogs eat gizzard.

I saw the city
            changed,
set up like laboratory glassware,
like amines of herring brine,
the malic acid of the sea buckthorn,
glass-enclosed prescription balance,
steel and agate, Fabrik Köln,

a physics clear as alcohol,
La Vita Nuova, I hardly knew.

Creditors dined at the Cliquot Club.
They read the papers. Trade changed.
Their horses died, the big-bellied.
Their dogs slept in the steam heat.

An ambulance with modest
glass doors and a silver cross
keeps night watch.

A surgeon.
Delicate nickel-plated
instruments are laid on trays.

Illuminated on the operating table
                    naked glassblowers,
gunsmiths, barbers, clerks, importers,
old men from hotels, pink and tailored,
naphtha-smelling Irish priests,
cravat-and-boy face of the movie usher,
Frankel, Shmulik, Old Country watchmakers.

Then a white horse in the park,
Cigars and politics.
The city wrapped in cellophane,
an act—born eggshape
                    twisted like Ugolino.
One sea-water,
                one circulatory system
of man observing his magnificent urea.

A Dry Thomas

The charisma of Mr. Eliot
                        floats
on plenary light
                from Bloomsbury
to everlasting,
                for his holy spirit
was conceptually right.

20

Lying in Bed on a Summer Morning

How pleasant are the green
and brown tiles
of my neighbor's roof.
The branches of his elm tree
stretch across
and make a delightful
composition,
          the angle
of the roof
          the exact plane
which the branch needs
to be interesting.
Le mot juste? la branche juste!

And you, my dark spruce,
dominate the left side
of this composition.
You are clannish but authentic
and stand, uncompromising,
for the family of trees.

And all at once the early birds
all break out chirping
as when the bidding opens
on the stock exchange.
          Then one,
the long sweet warble
of a finch.
          Oh stay!
And then a chant from down the street,
two boys triumphant,
very small in thick thick glasses:
"We got a bird nest! We got a bird nest!"

21

But a younger brother,
left behind and clobbered
when the mother was not looking
saw his chance to singsong back
(ah, sweet revenge):
                    "But
a woodpecker didn't make that nest!"

And now I come to you, sky.
What is there between us?

For one, I love El Greco,
who was your painter.

Your blue is clear
as on the first day.

In your presence I am man
and feel as if I
                    could live forever.

Questions for Jennifer Ebin,
My Eighteen-Month-Old Granddaughter

Whose face is so fair
that her eyes look blue
though they are brown

and bubbles fresh
and sits in me
like a nut in a shell?

Who knows, are we a galaxy
or a familial cell?

In what Sumerian babble,
wrapped for the night in a dark crib,
does she re-enact the hilarious encounter
with her body in the warm bath
and dada the dog
and bapa the grandpa
and her first complete sentence:
"Bye bye bubble down drain?"

Who is the inane reader
holding up one finger,
asking, "How much is one finger?"

Who bleeds for time
yet runs with her
into a bubble
and finds it interesting?

He who is without onus probandi,
a grandfather!
(grandmothers will have to write
their own riddles).

Young Girl

on her way to the beach,
walking daintily in bare feet
to avoid the stones.

Titania's gauze
forms a cute skirt,
                    so short
it takes the breath away
and opens in front
to admit man
to her shapely legs
                    walking brightly
in inexorable scissor movement
through his child taboos.

At thirteen she
already swings her hips,
ostensibly to keep her balance,
and re-enacts the secret
of man's bed.
She smiles and shoots
implacable seduction
straight into the eyes.

A nimbus envelops her girdle.

Oh stay!

Disclose your meaning.

"I like the way you look at me.
The lubricities of your mind."

Hold it, grandpa.
From where I stood, it sounded more like
"How delightful
that you noticed my new swimming suit!
It makes me feel like a woman."

Touché!

But was it so far out to imagine
that in the safety of that dark,
rather old-fashioned, sensitive
homuncio look in the poet's eyes,
having only a moment,
she let the panther out
of her pubic lair
to show that she was nubile,
and became ionized herself?

It was a great day
for Patrick Henry
                    Junior High.

Such bitter-sweet discombobulations
in a moment turn men into Pierrots.

The Husband

There were many things
to watch:
              her teeth,
her heart,
              her weight.
her nipples,
              the albumen
in her water.

Finally her shoes
no longer fit her.
So he said, "Your looks
are not gone.

Take it easy.
You'll know
when your time comes
and will not have a Mongolian
idiot in the taxi.

We'll make it
even if I have to tie
the cord myself."

A Poem to My First-Born

I felt
the foetus stir
a foot
below my wife's
breast.

Is that any reason
to wake
the neighbors
with my shouting
until they protest,
"What's the matter
with the silly ass?"

Well, I am
the provider.
Let us get to know
each other.

The Father

I find among my notes
a crayon drawing
of a prancing pony
with pink and blue legs
and an upright endpiece
looking more like a black
bush than a tail.
The eyes are bull's eyes,
fierce white in a black ring.
There is no mistaking
two rudimentary horns,
pink also, protruding
from the forehead.
This is mitigated
by an assortment of red
and pink cookie-shapes
spangled over the pony's coat
and by a green box
saddled to his middle
with a pink ribbon
on which you had printed
when you were four years old:
HAPPY BIRTHDAY,
forgetting that on the other side
you had scribbled
MOMMY IS A DOPE!

Which reminds me of the pact
you tried to make
after announcing you were
"sipping sopping soaking wet."

"When I do something bad,
I'll tell you how to punish me."

27

No dice.

Animal charm?
                    Viz.,
"Here, little egg,
I want to eat you!"

I'll never understand
what made you say:
"I'm tired
of being four.
I want to be five."

Where to, Mistress Quickly?

The Dead Father

Let me be an old dog in a corner
or a pair of favorite slippers
                              by your bed
and hear again about your early life
and have you care for me forever.

The Old Man

At first the hair
grew thicker on his chest
and stomach
and thinner on the top
of his head.

Then gray appeared
along the right side
of his chest.

One day he looked
into the mirror
and saw thick gray
hair in his nostrils.

Then he was willing
to concede
that age had come.

The old man
took his teeth out
from the water glass
and cut himself
a little sausage.

As a boy
he had been in such a hurry
to get older.
Now he felt younger
than ever.

To a Collie Pup

Nobody had to show you
where the sun is
or that my back
could serve the same purpose
as a tree.

Why, you are hardly old enough
to know the difference
between your tail and a shadow,
yet the warm radiator
and your bowl of water
are already old friends.

The way you look up at me
with a saint in each eye,
one would never suspect
that you chase birds and chickens
and steal stale bread
from the neighbor's trashcan.

Lay off, you beggar,
I just fed you
and took you walking.

Go spring
into the autumn leaves.
Nuzzle and roll
as if there were nothing
in the whole wide world
but fun.

How is it
that you play
with my shoelace
and understand so well
how to love me?

30

For this you shall have
The key to my bedroom
and the degree
of master of arts.

Shore Line

We speak of *mankind.*
Why not *wavekind?*

Barrel-chested military water
rushes in a mass
to break the shore earth
into *stonekind* under water.

Pphlooph pphlooph
                         the waves grope
indistinctly for the shore.

As delicate
              as a butterfly
along a cheek
              a boat with white
and orange sail appears.
A small boy in a life-belt
sits in front and looks ahead
with all his might.
              His father steers,
attached like a shaft
to his son's safety
and the sail's management.

A sunfish thrown back by a fisherman
lies drowned and pitching.
The eyes are white in death.

This is the raw data.
A mystery translates it
into feeling and perception;
then imagination;
finally the hard
inevitable quartz
figure of will
                    and language.

Thus a squirrel tail flying
from a handlebar
unmistakably establishes
its passing rider
as a male unbowed
                    in a chipper plume.

Jig, You Wine Bums

Bite the hard cool
                    apple of the air!

The season of muscatel has come
when the squirrel runs
up the tree fornicating
and the deer bolts

and man reaches
for his calking gun
and paint brush

and the middle aged hiker
throws his shoulders back.
Look at him go!

32

This is lavender and rose
time in drawers

when the sun is cooler but more blinding
and the maple leaves distil its light
into a cheerful red liqueur.

Now, wine bums,
The winter is long.
Elixir falls from the air,
and even the misanthrope
                                    's eye twinkles
in the commonplace.

Who Said There Was No Humor
in Latin Manuscripts?

A young monk
searching for what
had never yet
been seen
in Europe
came across
this declaration,
which he copied
in a bold hand:
"Leo the Lion
will stand up
to anybody!"

Laokoon

We are not given many moments
of biological integrity.

Our pasteboard tragedy is not the wasteland
but the faked stance and the forced feeling.

Therefore, thinker, do not be Laokoon of *I*
nor take the pose of constitutional loneliness.

Above all, do not try to be a prophet.
You will be caught
                        moving your stage props around
for maximum apocalyptic effect.

You

in whom distrust lies
            like a gallstone
and desire grows up aching
            like a sharp tooth,
there are times your courage
            rises over all
and knows no high airs
            or aloofness.

Then I plant myself near you
and swear I shall never leave.

To the Non-Political Citizen

You choose your words too carefully.
Are you afraid of being called agitator?

Every man is entitled to his anger.
It's guaranteed in the Constitution.
Every man is also entitled
to his own opinion and his own death,
his own malice and his own villainy.
But you spend too much time goosing.

The Declaration of Pierrot

I will put my purity away now
and find my art in other men
before I end up like a candle
in the bedroom of an old maid.

I am tired of wearing out my seat
regretting I was not Shakespeare
and trying to make my reading
approach an age like memory
a mother's face, restoring dimly
here a tooth and here a smile

or plucking a lute
and singing a madrigal.

This is no time
to be looking backward.

Country People Never Learn

They are the same everywhere.
This one driving
his cart along the Danube,
why should he give up
his good sheep
and his open fields
and the sight of goats
on the Carpathians
for a strange war
in a strange land?

To an Anti-Semite

So you fought for the Jews
in the last war
and have become a patriot again!

Why you thick-skulled liar,
as impossible to offend
as to trust with an order,

you were never within
three thousand miles
of the front.

You fought the war
in Camp McKinley,
cleaning stables

and stealing out
into the moonlight
with the kitchen maids.

The Founding of New Hampshire

A slender plank above a waterhole
planted on end to meet my wants,
I hear its whisper in the stock.
It does not sway a hair's breadth.

Another stake driven in and well shaved
points against the light from the layout.
The maple fits upon the joist like a flower,
                              a picked beam,
a great wood to plane and saw.

I tell my wife the walls are up,
the strips nailed at snug right angles,
                    the floors are oiled.
The Yankee poles are almost columns.

Braced against a gloomy magnitude,
I loiter civil on my soles and buffeted,
killing time in these traditions.

Are the woodsmells getting sweeter
or the broker working at my back
so that all the concord in the timber
can not warm this house?

Americana 1

The settler cleaned and loaded his rifle carefully
before a warm hearth, examining every part
before taking out over hostile Indian country
with his dog at his side.

The philosopher asked, "Why?
If your time has come, you'll die anyway."

"I know that, but it may be the Indian's time."

Americana 2

The Lord came in a vision to the hardshell screamer
and revealed the letters G P C, which told him:
    Go Preach Christ!
Thus rammed, he led a raid on the idealists,
charging Communism and dishonor to the American eagle.

What saith the defendants?
        "G P C sounds more like Go Pick Cotton
and reminds us of the time the preacher rode up
    to the deacon's house
saying, "The Lord told me in a dream last night
to get a load of corn from your crib."
"The Lord then must have changed His mind,"
replied the deacon, reaching for his long rifle,
"because He told me this morning not to let you have it."

Americana 3

On Washington's Birthday Yancey the haberdasher
ran a full-page ad under a banner headline
in deference to the boy who could not tell a lie:
IT'S TIME WE QUIT FOOLING YOU

                                   Yancey's had a false front.
It was ten feet shorter inside than out.
To correct this, he was knocking walls down, moving
    fixtures,
putting in new lights and introducing a new heating
    system
in order to give his customers the opportunity
to be seduced by accessories of the finest quality.

Atta boy, merchant! Down the hatch!

One time in Boot Hollow Little Ab Yancey challenged
    Foggy Dell
and his companions Homer Bullteeter and Slappy Hen-
step.
Crowing like cocks they accepted the challenge
and flapped their wings.
                    Then Ab rose up and neighed
                    like a horse:
"I'm the yellow flower of the forest
all brimstone but the head and that's aquafortis"
and rode them down like lightning through a crab-apple
    orchard.

"We're satisfied," they conceded. "You're a beauty!"

Americana 4

The whole town used to gather around
the four bands in the four saloons on the corner.

Okey Poke used to tend bar behind a diamond
      sunflower stickpin
and the gambler Ed Mochez, who left a hundred and ten
      suits
when he died,
                played every hand of poker like a tiger.

People in and out day and night,
all raising simultaneous barrelhouse cain.

Where is Willie the Pleaser?
                Always women running after him,
that sweetback man kind of strutting with it
in a very mosey walk from down the river
            called Shooting the Agate.

One day a boy picked up a flute and started right in
      playing it.
Showed everybody what *is* a flute!

Walked over to a saxophone
and damn if he didn't start making the thing just talk!

"Go, my son, and riff it through the land,"
                and he went

through manhood in his comic little hat.
He'd walk out on the stage and say, "I'd like to
      introduce my band,"
and introduced the musicians to each other.

Then he'd step back, tilt his horn
and blow a high note of emancipation.
Then the reeds would liquefy and move out,
far out on a mellow riff,
                        and his trombones
peppered dirty notes to make it real,
and church rocked!
                        Not a chick in town
was safe until the blues cut him down.

The origin of the blues?
                        Always been.
Some poor hustling woman feeding her fancy Dan
                        in the servants' room.
Some poor guy playing a mysterious bass
fatherless figure on his trombone,
sometimes braying on it like a jack
being the porter in the barber shop.

Some underground Jupiter grieving:
Lord, your servant Juba lives in hog slop.
Give this offchild your medicinal herbs,
root of the master weed, Peter's roots,
and May apple and sweet William.

The origin of the blues?
                        The white hero!

Americana 5

As it gets on in years
the third generation
feeling lonely with its children
goes into its darkroom
and develops a picture

of cattle lumbering in from the timbered pasture
at the end of a summer's day a century ago
their bags heavy with milk

planting the acre north
of the hoghouse to sweet corn
for late eating with fresh country butter

families visiting from a hundred miles
singing under a shade tree.

Where the road forks at the red barn
and the oak tree has a knot hole
on its north side
the old ones feel at home,
hoeing weeds in a little garden
and marveling how things grow
the corn having jumped a foot
over the Fourth of July weekend.

Here four-square on historic legs
on all sides bounded
by (how is this capitalized?)
God and hard work
stands the Nineteenth Century.

Florida

of bright cities
                and citrus,
Florida of coral
and sawgrass pointing

                    straight north
and hotels full
                    of ocean air
and little garment manufacturers
                    with retired eyes
and broads and bartenders
                    (on the make)
soaking in your orange clef,

of Negro cabins
                    with the cotton picker's
deep slave voice
                    imploding
into warm hosannahs,
the other Florida
                    of patient Africanus.

Irish Fantasy on the Eighth Century

A plain word with Gaelic associations
summoned me to this gathering place
for holy men from a river holm of lambs.

Mercenaries from the great fort Lissaghmore
and harpers and bards from Finscotha
where flowers are pressed into wine,
and peddlers from the cuil of ants Coolnamagh joined us,
and weavers from the village of the virgin saint Cocca,
and druids from the tree place Cranalagh,
tanners from Ballinduff, the town of dark men,
potters from the clear little stream Finglas,
thieves and gamesters from the mouth of the yellow ford

43

where the great battle was fought between two O'Brians,
farmers from the small level places
and kings and queens grieving on a walnut isle in Yeats.

The work of women spreading flax out,
malting barley on the lake shore
and hawking Balscadden herrings in twigs
made this a darling place.

There was a church in shrubs and blackthorn
here for every fish in the Liffey.
The ram leaped
                    and the seal disported on small rocks
and birds and geese cackled in the glen
and Castlekirk was built in one night by a cock and a hen.

The land was black rock and white weir.
There was an abundance of meadows
and oakgroves for pigs
                    and plains for heifers
and moors for red grouse.

Forts were built in oat fields
and the medium of exchange
                    was the yearling heifer.

The aged leaders made the strong-balled galloglas
                    with thick red chest hair,
whose obligations were designated in the law,
protectors of St. Patrick and the state.

They lie in Saintfield with the little men
whose blarney, like the little word I started with,
dug no potatoes
                    but appeared
to circumscribe adversity.

Four Characters and a Place
in The Merchant of Venice

1. Four Characters

Antonio, a special breed of existential cat:
a Christian, merchant, friend,
yet suffers from an enigmatic melancholy.
Spits on the Jew.

Nerissa, a gnat who'd make an outstanding critic.
Pricks a literary convention before the bubble
has a chance to be launched.
A Sancho in Quixotic clothes.

Gratiano, a hot head.
If there are Jews in Venice,
let them lock their doors.
This man will hate them
and be itching for a fight.
Prick him in his little finger
and he becomes the very foreskin of an anti-Jew.

Shylock. Is it possible a man can be so real
in the conventions of a tale of love,
he has the smell of boiled beef on his breath?

"The Jew," says Gobbo, "is the very devil
incarnation"
                    and fun to taunt and defy.

Therefore after Shylock lost his child
and fortune, "all the boys in Venice follow him,
Crying his stones, his daughter, and his ducats,"
for did not Shakespeare give the signal
of impending villainy himself
by calling Shylock sixty times *"the Jew"*?

What should one say? That the age
had not heard of the man of Sinai yet
who baked compassion into moral order?
Should one not say, this family man
had tenderness and ancient humor
built in like the glow-worm's light?
That it appears that Shylock is an afterbirth
left by the monk's dame that begat the Devil,
the one who wrote the special dossier on the Jew
which split the Middle Ages like a lightning
bolt with this syllogism:
Man was born in sin. Only Christ can save.
Christ is spurned by Jews. Therefore Jews
are sinister or perhaps not really men.

So when Antonio's bond was forfeited
and the gracious duke said
in his best melodious voice:
"We all expect a gentle answer, Jew!"
Shylock rode implacability to the end.

But so did Lear
                    and there were tears for Lear!

But we forget this is an early play,
a midsummer night's dream stabbed
by the long black caftan'd quiddity
of an earlier Italian villain,
                              before Barabbas!
that England had not seen a real
unbaptized Jew in three hundred years,
having banished these proto-bankers
(not before reneging on the notes due).

Yet Shylock is a stronger brew than dreams
are made of, straightforward as his ducats,
yet not so real as flesh and blood.

Doggett, a famous low comedian of his day,
played him as a sharper.

"But suppose," as one apologist for Shylock wrote,
"that Shylock had subjected Antonio
to the same indignities, what would be thought?"

"Our sympathies are with him," Hazlitt wrote.
"He is honest in his vices"
and the only way to play him
is as Kean did with a "terrible energy"

or with scorn for Gratiano, as Irving did,
hurling a thunderbolt of understatement
when the trial was over and he said,
**"I pray you give me leave to go from hence,
I am not well,"** and "walked away
to die in silence and alone"
or like Mansfield on **"I am not well"**
to gut himself

        or chuck it all
and outfit Shylock as a low comedian
in pants pouched like a kangaroo
with gravel voice and sad, repeated
pratfalls on enormous pancake shoes,
but keep the poetry in Venice
in a cubist blue-and-white stage.

2. Belmont

a country of the mind
held subject by the harmony of friendship
and the perdurable vows of lovers
whose perpetual desires pump systole and diastole.

Chafing like a captive princess,
a fifteen-year-old suburban Jewess, Jessica,
fled with her father's jewels and a monkey
and eloped to Belmont with a neoplatonic youth,
a handsome nonentity,

and the crusader Godfrey of Bouillon
drove the Jews of Jerusalem into the Synagogue
and burned it down.
    And Shylock said,
*"Let not the sound of shallow fopp'ry enter
my sober house."*

   *"In such a night
Medea gathered the enchanted herbs
that did renew old Aeson"*

and in the sacked ghetto
two men wrestled for a pot.

   *"In such a night
stood Goebbels with a willow in his hand
upon the wild sea banks"*

      and the dead Jew lay
face up, a dog chewing on his hat.

All "vanish into thin air"
but the heavenly bodies which the ear
of Shakespeare heard in English,
the lovers buzzing in a hive of small acts
and the revellers materializing
into bone and gristle when they meet a Jew
who grounds their euphoric charge.

All their ploy is jell'd in clearest amber,
but the Jew remains in Gratiano's craw.

"What's that for?"
     "To bait fish withal!"

The Lobster

Eastern Sea, 100 fathoms,
green sand, pebbles,
broken shells.

Off Suno Saki 60 fathoms,
gray sand, pebbles,
bubbles rising.

Plasma-bearer
and slow-
motion benthos!

The fishery vessel *Ion*
drops anchor here
                    collecting
plankton smears and fauna.

Plasma-bearer, visible
sea purge,
            sponge and kelpleaf.
Halicystus the Sea Bottle

resembles emeralds
and is the largest
cell in the world.

Young sea horse
Hippocampus twenty
minutes old—

nobody has ever
seen this marine
freak blink.

It radiates on
terminal vertebra
a comb of twenty

upright spines
and curls
its rocky tail.

Saltflush lobster
bull encrusted swims

backwards from the rock.

Ships

One o'clock. A rainy night.
The sea air darkens on the wheelhouse.
The binnacle glows.
                    "Ho there, ho!"
The whole hull of **The Frisco Cross,**
a twin-screw tanker, lights up.
                    "Who are you?"
A dry face.
            The chronometer tilts.
"All lights burning brightly, sir."

A little river steamer from the tariff frontiers,
twelve cabins and a white light on the masthead,
with its house flag and a freeboard of 6″,
                                        boys
running with mates' receipts and bills of lading,
carries kilderkin imperial kegs and stingo firkins.

The great turbo-electric ocean liner, fire insured,
has circulating ice water swift for the belly,
and anchor hooks and foreign mail.

Unswerving Marine

This is in the wind:
that an old seaman
                    paces the planks again
as his weedy hull parts
                    the saltseries inaudibly.
What ho! She carries full sails
and the chant of the grog-quaffers
                    in an important manner.
But there is no port
and the wind is distracted
                    from her simple stern
like the mind.
Continuously the undefined plane
                              emerges
in the form of a ship,
her nose speeding in the brine-ellipsis,
routing the shads and alewives
                    from her shaping way.
And the wind
              and the mind sustain her
and there is really
                    no step upon the gangway,
nothing but the salt deposits
                              of the open.

Early American Chronicle

A cutter risen from the mollusks, it is a god
with a god carved on the stempiece,
arriving in Detroit with Jesuits,
canvas, cable, chain, tar, paint . . .
feluccas, pinnaces, and brigantines
with mainsail hauled out on a little tackle.

Here cometh not the King of France
nor the Secretary for the Latin Tongue
nor the Lord High Butler of England
with coronation jewels.

I spit on them al.
They have broken me for the last time.
I lie on the high poop al the night
with open eye, with wenches, singing
in radium like Chaucer and the smale fowles.

A sail in Atlantis in the morning, a Sappho
of a sloop slapping the buss ship **London**
white and anchored as a living clam.

Night Thoughts

After the jostling on canal streets
and the orchids blowing in the window,
I work in cut glass and majolica
and hear the plectrum of the angels.

My thoughts keep dwelling on the littoral
where china clocks tick in the cold shells
and the weeds slide in the equinox.

The night is cold for love,
a chamber for the chorus
and the antistrophe of the sealight.

Fluteplayers from Finmarken

How keen the nights
were, Svensen.
Not a star out,
not a beat of emotion
in the humming snowhull
(now and then an aweful swandive).

It seemed ordained then
that my feet slip on the seal bones
and my head come down suddenly
over a simple rock-cistvaen,
grief-stricken and archwise.
Thereon were stamped
the figures of the noble women
I had followed with my closed eyes
out to the central blubber
of the waters.

(There is not a pigeon
or a bee in sight.
My eyes are shut now
and my pulse dead as a rock).

The Swedish mate says he recalls
this fungoid program
of the mind and matter
where the abstract signals

     to the abstract
and the mind directs

     a final white lens
on the spewing of the waterworm
and the wings of the midsea.

It was not clear what I was after
in this stunted flora
and husky worldcold
until the other flutes arrived. . . .
four masters musing
from one polar qualm to another.

Brewing Night Herbs

Under the oak leaves
you and I lie
far from the eternal hearths
and animate the ideal
with internal passion.

The evening softly falls
on house and herb
and all the boughs
and heights fall
on us as we lie
under the oak leaves
brewing night herbs.

Figures in an Ancient Ink

In the dense scopes
Jupiter progenitor,
perfumed a Christian,
fishes in the reefs
with ancient weights
or sometimes wanders
an apocryphal white goat.

And Hrothgar the wandering scop,
heartrover among your fathers,
sails the North Sea
with a load of deerhides
                    and bird feathers
and two thousand tods
                    of whalebone for the Danes.

And Saracen physicians
under a pecan tree
discuss the heart.

These unconnected images no doubt
once represented agents
and fellows bearing yokes,
but that is not the way
they speak to me.

I made them
but took away their speech
and gave them instead a precious
patina of ancient associations.
That is how they got their mystery
and speak to me.

What, am I in love then
with my own images, an Onan
wrapped in their protective strangeness?
shrinking from what failure?

Strange that such a patina should be
more durable than the actual Hrothgar!

Origins

In the salt warp
was the plasma,
in the springhead
and the sulphurous water.

Jupiter the sire hawk
flew through Athens.
Then the Greeks sang
and the wings turned
through the light.

We sat upon a stone
with happy records,
shipping kelp and sulphur
through the islands.

Athens was a hawk.

And Corinth was once
a pedestal for wrestlers
in classical shorts.
What method in their manner!

Shall we say the gods
with lights behind us
have broken wind
in a changing system?

Yesterday behind the olive boughs
they seemed so lucid!

Send us again, O gods,
peppers and poppyseed,
porphyry and white cocks.

After a thousand years,
                    behold
the apple blossoms of the new world;
the early grapes;
the young man's cartograph
on which appears an arrow
pointed north to heaven.
There the gentle still idealize,
the heart is lighter,
and the Cross attends.

But we pass obscurely
from post to sleep,
opening the constructions
of the virtuous and loghouse
Puritans of Massachusetts.
They planted radishes
and hailed the Savior
spreading his alarming
feathers over the pickets.

A country house in April
after a thousand years:
poor headpiece,
you are unhappy.

Buy yourself some alcohol for winter
and a squirrel rifle
                        for Sunday morning.
You too will juggle
rabbits, eggs, bananas,
physical and resolute.

Tumblers in the nebula,
is not every man
his own host?

A Journey Away

1.

The wayfarer met the passerby
in death's champaign of flowers.
As the lint blew through their skulls
they spoke discreetly of the next world,
of the slobland to the left
and the aweful coprolite above.
The words were impressive and muted.
Suddenly the one preoccupied
with his obsolete luetic eyeball
made a meaningless aside
in keeping with the serious scene.

2.

I dreamed last night
that I was married.
I was scared, the woman
being very young, with green
stones in her garter.

She looked upon me wistfully
                    and said:
I was a taxi dancer
with a sweetheart on a fishing smack.
I perceive by these pains
that I am condemned to die.

From Okeanos sprang
                    her hot breath.
Her image is an ancient blue glass,
                    so subtle.
It reminded me
of one I had not seduced.
She was brushing out her hair
before the mirror.

I should have been arranging
the white poppies in the window
with the coriander.

3.

You were traveling through Delos
when the end came.

On the esplanade at Cannes
the awnings suddenly
went black before me.
I was carried to the belvedere
of Villa Policastro.

In the evening
in the sight of blood and bandages
I lay there like a dressed fowl.
On a marble seat
                    above the Ligurian
another evening.

An ideal
like a canary
singing in the dark
for appleseed and barley.

Something also from the laurel,
a tiny arsis.

4.

We climbed the stairs,
the white dress flowing
from the lady's sides.

She turned the pottery lamp.

How shall I wear you,
center crown stone,
great blue solitaire of sentiment?
They will say I am Jewish.

She took my hand and pointed out
the men's shops with terrazzo floors,
the city desks, the shoe windows,
the Carlton waiters with a canapé
of coral lobster, 666 for colds
and fevers, the suburban shore drive,
the old man hammering in the doll shop.

So light the room, like air
about a willow branch.
A glass stands on the golden table.
Prints of St. Marks, The Bargello,
Mme. LeBrun and her Daughters.
A glass vase with a spinning stem.

"This is my daughter Sue."

She sat adamic as with jug
and towel for a painter.

A young girl's study: lace
and nimbus from the east.

She played a classical pianoforte,
clef-wandering sweet pinna tremolo,
a Chippendale in a dominoes étude:
the Bird pirriko pirriko prrrk
     ia ia
the leghorn rustling in the brush,
the creek between the rockshelves.
Nancy with a bunch of wet grapes.

5.

A light in the morning
crystallized upon the crest
entranced the virgin.
There the fawn stood,
hunted, bated, sensitized
and sainfoin breath,
being, unknown to himself,
a cornea of light.

6.

Sea-kin,
we have broken away.
Our hearts are grounded
in the waterways.
Our butts foam
in the current like a keel.

We pray
that our wings may blaze
in the sterling course.

7.

The black arena bull bleeds
                              in the neck.
The ladies are gone.
                    I throw a rose
upon the black loins.
                    Tomorrow
another bullfight
                    and the gall irk
of cafard and skeptic.

Keep the whisky from me.

The Heifer

After the bath she touched her hair
with Orange Leaf and smiled.

"Henry is gone. Who are you?"

Fumous ashwood violins
all night made bright da capo
constant as specific gravity.
So the umbrellas were put away.
We were together on yachts and beaches,
breakfasts on the ocean,
taxis through the Brandenburger Tor.

"Tell me. Who are you?"

I am son
of a Hungarian peasant
who fled military service
where the sheep graze
                    under the Carpathians
and the cheese hangs on the rack
and black bread and potato soup
                    was the family meal,

who came to America
                    to a steel mill
and a single room
                    in a boarding house.

I am he who lost
his father's simple power
to touch and smell
untouched by philosophy . . .
the inexpugnable integrity
of a heifer licking its nose . . .
forever lost,
                    forever lost.

The Status Quo

It is good to be here.
This city is a shell forced open
and the foreign matter
                    shining sea-forced pearl.

But the people who made this city
out of sand and petroleum oil,
domestic sulphite, Old Paper,
Newsroll Contract, short wool,
kip, Ohio & Pa. fleeces,

63

fine up-river rubber,
tank plates, wire nails,
China wood oil, mason's lime,
pine roofers, spruce lath,
basket-fired Japan tea,
white Singapore pepper,
burlap, Newfoundland cod, etc.

the people who made it all,
weep, rising from their base
like a single stone figure
with head bowed,
for the city belongs to its creditors,
chairmen of boards dining at the Club
the city belongs to its newspapers
and its lawyers.

The Wedding

Between the two gold
vases of Bermuda lilies
go the egg-shaped

feelings of a man
fearing son and whore,
feeling his heart

peeled from its mesentery
and washing and beating
on a board between the organ

and the bride's gown,
and his memory touched
with invitation and ideal.

Equipoise

This commanding
young head
which outshines
its antecedents,
        magnificent
and mortal
compound on a tower,
burns
    with the cautery
of affection.

Therefore, flash
and magnify
the canons of perfection
        in an ankle,
in the waistline,
        in the private
morals of this lady.

Hold before our eyes,
with wits divided,
an abstract of every
        man's spring.

Hold an atomweight of hawthorn.
Do not blow
it off the point of concept,
for the masterweights of spring
equipoise like jewels.

Handel

The piccolo of heaven
      ed the scales.
climb

A blue cusp
      s
       a
        n
         k

like gauze.

The book of dawn
         fell
open on my brow,
a chronicle of the eternal
          virgin
graciously held
by archimandrite hands.

I
  w
  a
 s
    divisions
like the z d a
       o i c

and from the blue
the icelight of an
      afternoon.

Song

Turning as from an instrument
the faces open like a choir
shining from the pillars
in quadragesimal sentiment.

The spiritual eyes assume
a coronation music.
One by one the fluent breaths
respond in the gloom.

Briefly the eyes uphold
their acclamations.
Briefly the voices touch,
the eyes grow cold.

Return, Sweet Ladies

with streamers blowing
                         in our English.
Preceded by the favored birds,
the clouds escort you
                         with an ancient program
while the lonely sharp-eyed one
weeps a moment
                         in adoration.

Paraguay

In the early hours
                the lovebirds
colonized the palm.

We were looking for a totem.

In the east
where the sun deflects the falcons
from their sea positions
and the Indian smells
we found a frere
with no cathedral
but the daisies in May,
living on milk and wafers,
with the cross in one hand
and anatomy in the other.

Range in Ancient China

Winter shakes
the iced plums
by the lonely wall.

There are no toys
like walking
in this paktong garden.

Trembling Acolyte

Blond youth,
make hue of sober days.
Burn like an actor star.

The mountain sinks of void
make sound you knew
while dreaming
what the chords of cosmos are.

Some nights tremble
strange strings
in your head
and across
the love of evening
                platforms
evoke her tread.

The dusk returns her Greek
prose figure
while the oxwagons of thought
trek out to space.

Can you not move or speak?
Her hair is basalt
music,
       light and metre.

Wild fowl, apes and cavemen
wait with you
through the starstream
             for a woman.

The January of a Gnat

Snow panels, ice pipes, house the afternoon
whose poised arms lift prayer with the elm's antennae.
She has her wind of swift burrs, whose spiel is gruff,
scanning the white mind of the winter moon
with her blank miles. Her voice is lower
than the clovers or the bassviol of seastuff.

So void moons make a chaste anabasis
across the stalks of star and edelweiss
while Volga nixies and a Munich six
o'clock hear in the diaphane the rise
of one bassoon.
                          So the immense frosts fix
their vacant death, bugs spray the roots like lice.
High blizzards broom the cold for answer
to their ssh of vapors and their vowel ooo.

Flora and the Ogre

Let her quince knees sag
and the toy arcs of the dew
and daisy
guide her mild feet,
her torso is no more to me
than the woodcut of a nun.

In a peignoir snowing to her ankles
she paces the movement
of sun and dark.
Her step is like the pulse of lilies.

All motion blurs the scented yaw of her skirts
(linen like the subsiding of labials,
like the undertow in the veins).

While the three tenses
faltered between her painful thighs,
a wind of scarves rose.

Will no briny thunderbrunt
or green chill
deliver me?

Fantasy

One must have sullen wits
to foot the jungle
like another darkness
because of *heimweh*
and an air spiced
                          with big fruit.
The bamboos shiver
and the tattooed bird caws
to the rose-chafer in the moon.
It's mumbo-jumbo banging a tom-tom,
his black feet straggling
in the thrum of oil palms.
Ivory hunters with a tree mask
Come up the river.
There are many apes.
In the tiger country
beyond the grain,
                          the black one
rolls her pubes.

71

The continent is waterbound
                    and one
outside the singer in the shack,
and Sambo, fat cigar
                    in heaven,
chucks the white dice
gravely with a black crow.

Extracts from a Private Life

1.

Your second cousin, an obscure
                    cigar-maker from Smyrna,
impresses me with tom thumb news.
The words are blunt
                    and throw a sour limelight.
He regrets the way your eye
                    gluts on the dancing girls
like an oyster in the head of Bacchus.

But his hands too explore this woman's calf,
his hide lights up
                    above her loincloth
like a white spark by an epitaph.

2.

Witnessed the atom of the element boron
at zero in a classic crucible. . . .
the sub-beat of the summer's metronome
(the organheat of Fez prefigured
by a salved cosmopolis of koran men). . . .

the birdclef of Manhattan Limited
(a mudhen in a shooting gallery).

Picked up the signet of these hanging contras
and baled into words.
                              The pince-nez spied
across the astral valance
                              in straight mercurial lines.

3.

My house lights thunder
                    like a tungsten pigeon,
and a leafshadow takes cover in the wainscot
                    like a hound.
I lock my doors against the beastly draughts.

The light above the chessmen spoke:
I am Avalokiteshvara Matsyendranatha,
                    Lord of Fishes.
Your haunches shall be buried tomorrow
                    by finished skeptics,
like big god pater Jove magnificent.

4.

My wants are like the sparrows of a shepherd,
bony and dark on every shoulder,
                    and the hair and thumbs,
flying in a beautiful electric order.

I hear my ear-pulse trot out
                    like a horse on asphalt,
and the watch under my pillow singing
                    like Venetian glass.

73

5.

Lay down the book
    and match your wits
against this bird
    when day breaks.

Basic black salts of the mind,
go the way of earth
    and women
into lyric matters.

Homage to Wallace Stevens

1.

Clear me with this master music
when the coryphée skips on the oak floor
and the clouds depress me like the lower keys.
This drama sets the clocks of epigram.

The grave salons with lines of peridot
in the interior and cairngorm pomp
attest refinements of the clavichord.

The pieces are the will of shadows
and the person in the polished doorway
feels the dark mask of his chamber sentiments.

These are the privacies behind the mask
but they are not the manners of a boy
who blows his French horn, smiles at twelve o'clock
and sips the old port from the hostess' shoe.

This etiquette is stranger than the fellowship
which turns an apricot liqueur
and absinthe into innocence,
the bottles into happy unities
among the pie-eyed sobbing hooligans.

2.

I found Miss Levi in a plush repose,
counting the curves pitched in her portly mirrors
by seven bored and pygmy globes.
                              Her floors
were tourmaline supporting topaz standards.

Moist for the mouthing of mild platitudes,
here evenings passed Venetian glasses
and oak planes through green transitions.
Walnut backs diffused her satin cases.

She seemed faint, ecstatic
                         in her parlor sunsets,
stamping her wronged head on an old medallion.

The cisterns warbled the October rain
on afternoons.
                    We listened into green
designs of gloom like sleepers.
                              "Carl, I feel
the musings of profuse dim meistersingers."

Her meanings muffled dark interiors
which were an invocation to the sun.

"We mix with carbonates and corals
on pelagic passes where prawns sail
                              like passions.

Sea spiders hobble from my hair,
                              my eyes
shall twinkle into octagons of frost."

She heard a subway of demotic voices
scoffing at all unmusical dispassions.
Their basses settled into dantesque laughter
while icy faint buffoons professed rich prescience.

She said a lodge of hairless ponderers
would stand in choir while the infant dawns
poured tea, to chant the *aufklärung* of men.

Obsessions died among her sweet liqueurs
and pungent bottles.
                    She would stir cool coffee
and feel the messengers of void encroach.

While swallows chittered in the hush and light
and gulls idealized upon the sea,
a band of trumpets called a fierce refrain
for thud of blond divines from Palestine
whose footsteps drowned the ariette of birds.

And when her schoolmen passed like prophecy
and mighty infants, she could not affront
their high detachment with her bungled pathos.

Their white feet were an exhalation
of the lovely sin of death,
                          but they were bawds.

Exercises in Scriptural Writing

1.

The king shall understand
that Yahweh is
Lord of four kingdoms.
There is the kingdom of fire
that is the compend of His word.
And the kingdom of the earth
of which men say that it was Eden
(now but merchants).
And the kingdom of the air
where birds make offering to our Lord
for His benevolent attitude.
And finally there is the kingdom of water,
history of many winds
and sailors in their salty coffins.
                                Certainly
our Lord is like the apex in the south
and like the scepter of the north.

2.

Sandalwood comes to my mind
when I think of you
and the triumph of your shoulders.
Greek chorus girls came to me
in the course of the day
and from a distance
Celtic vestals too,
but you bring me the Holy Land
and the sound of deep themes
in the inner chamber.

I give you praise
in the language
of wells and vineyards.

Your hand recalls
the salty heat of barbarism.

Your mouth is a pouch
for the accents of queens.

Your eyes flow over
with a gentle psalm
like the fawn eyes
of the woodland.

Your black hair
plucks my strings.

In the foggy wilderness
is not your heart
a hermit thrush?

You are timeless
as the mirrors,
Jewess of the palm country,
isolate as the frost
on the queen of swans.
Now that I have seen
the royal stones and fountains
and the tetrarch's lovely swans,
I am satisfied that you are
a mindful of white birds
in the folly of an old Jew.

Because of the coral
of your two breasts

are the prophets angry,
but I have my lips upon them
and the song shall go on.

3.

At Stagira lies Saint Belle,
and there lies also the body of Aristotle.

And you shall understand
that her bones are anointed
with the gum of plum trees
and that all men are used
to attend her grave on Lent.

And men say that in her youth
she was led into a garden of Caiaphas
and there she was crowned
with the sweet thorn called barbariens.

But now this is no more
but a tablet seven cubits long
above her head
on which the title is written
in Hebrew, Greek and Latin
and the date
when it was laid in the earth.

And the body of Aristotle
stinks too in a casket
at Stagira, but the eyes
are in Paris in the king's chapel.
Yet the emperor of Almayne
claims he has them,
and I have oftentime seen them,
but they are greater
than those in Paris.

Conception

A plankwalk to the sea.

A smoked salmon on a line.

A ball of packing twine.

Everything in eggs and cubes.

As effortless and helpless
as if waiting for a corpse
with Jockey Club and heliotrope,
here comes the bride
with kewpie blue eyes
and a lighted brassiere.

It's a gay life
for the humorist
with a gardenia
in his lapel.

The Winter Garden

The musical revue
brings down the house.
Arms linked
to form a crocus,
the chorus girls

80

powdered and smiling
break it up
and climb into a bandbox
with a lovesong
and old-fashioned
romantic baskets
from the Emerald Isles.

Vitagraph

Out in God's country where men are men
the terror of Red Gap used to ride
on his Arizona roan.
He was called Goddam Higgins
and was said to have faith only in his gun,
his horse, and Denver Nan.

It turned out she was in cahoots with Gentleman Joe
and one day the two of them cleaned
the poor sucker out of his last red cent.

But it was the last time Gentleman Joe
hung his thumb into the armpit of his vest
and snickered behind his nibbled toothpick,
for a masked stranger showed up in the barroom
that night with his hand on his hip pocket.

Years later the Reverend Marcus Whitney
pitched his tent in town and Denver Nan
had her only chance to go straight
and made good and married Good Deed Higgins,
and three cheers for the Star Spangled Banner.

Revue 1

From Sinai to Killarney, a comic burst
with other harmonies and egopedes
wherein are found the shamrock and the redhead
and that beloved disjoint of merry woman,
lovely McCohen herself, the Lark.

Behind the baritone is love's own cottage
where the misfits look out on the health
and blossomtime of Plymouth Rock.

McCohen smiled.
                              "What eyes," lamented Jack,
"Their shadowboxing interests me.
Will she speak in orphic with the eyes
of insight and the plasma of elation?
or the voice of analytic hesitation?"

The myth and good form leave her.
                                                    Look!
They fly like the Pacific golden plover
and laughter follows like a dying whale.

Revue 2

They say in dreams they have a peetweet's view
of happy matters, but around them
and ahead stand fixtures of morality.
They scan these properties for some design
with a macabre elegant complexion,
but merely turn the screws of introspection;
turn and pick a ragtime on the strings

and drink a soda to a better day
when to a maiden's heart the ace of wits,
calligrapher and creeping microskeptic,
equipped like tourists with a worldly light,
will sing the blues of a gregarian.

Hi Ho the Merri-o. Fashion decrees
shaved jawbones for established gents
and sees them stripped to animal devotions,
swim in oceanic notions.

Leviathan and bulk of melancholy,
shine with us in miserable motions.

Superproduction

St. Louis songbirds in Atlanta.
Just a minute. This is romance.
Enter Nancy picking daisies.
Plughole sounds on the verandah.
All under the bedsheets rise.
The eyes thaw open and detect.

With the change in weather,
exposed and cooped in cold,
Nancy solicits your attention.
Nancy lies finished and deceived,
a sight to make your eyes fail
in the heated rooms, poisoned
by Rudolf's talcum manner.
Now love is slain and the well-groomed
lover is wanted in seven states.
Again perfidy clicks like a billiard ball
and bounds from unexpected cushions.

Nancy's beloved body travels
the long way in a silent box,
unscented, unattended
by rhythmical gloved gentlemen.

Voices demand a happy ending.
Let her find more comfortable quarters,
then, through any heated savior.

Characters

One of our brassy beefeaters
in grandstand on the continent
bares biceps to the gaping millions,
sinks shaft in market, pockets wheat,
holds cornucopia of cash.
Cheers heard before his private front
as he lands place with notables.
We call this tribute in a nutshell,
a miracle of entertainment.

Speaking of beaus sartorial,
perplexed young girl hands laugh to love-wise.
"I am a lovely, irresistible girl
of seventeen, with wondrous witching orbs.
Why do I blaze in my intangibles
like a mandolin romantic,
you, stable as the sterling?"

Wanted

Expert experiences black on white
by men who are all white from the midriff
to the arches through the lowest joints.
We train you in accepted imagery,
the sights of love, and other popular sports,
and keep your eyes peeled for the gems of gab.
Diction or fact, it's all one to the larynx . . .
The applicant is to be oriented,
a hustler from his collarbutton up,
upright and spry, a snotshooter
who spares no words or pleasant
whispers of address.
Report to us at once with sample pomp
and testimonies of urbanity.

Also a man to master mockery,
a spotlighter with strong intentions.

Sylvia

Trot out the negro singers, ladies, clowns,
and athletes to extol the morning.

Let the senator take out his dogs
to swim,
       and watch the sliding of the lake
below the smooth urns,
           ships cantabile
and oceanic near the stratospheric.

The fair man in the public eye
has read the life of simple Jesus,
undertaker of the West.

Sylvia hails him from a torpedo roadster.

He clears his title to her loins,
gets shaved and trimmed in her venereal parlors
where he rakes in on the wheel of love,
his standing polished like a dental mirror,
his old age lit up like a Christmas tree.

Frankfort and Bethlehem

This post card has the Christmas
spirit with its Lutheran
steeple between the hills,
its cow fence and its fir tree,
and a dirt farm in Thuringia.

Bright star,
unto you is born
this day a grub
                    in the addle.

Death Song

Young utopia of spring
                              greens,
hello,
        light up the towers
of the Whisky King,
behold the mints
and comics of the season
as the tempers light our reason
with penumbra and with chroma.

The Pollys in the Tenderloin
size up the town and vocalize.
The wise guy plucks a banjo string
for Polly's Irish eyes.

Only the fathers of the state
have public welfare up their sleeves.

Big-hearted Dick obeys the law
and trots around in chevron weaves
with dividends from anchored markets,
picking his manner from the facts

of God, the flying American.

Manifest and Lonely

The eyes are centered
on this lady's face
with flowers by her cheek,
a moment for the sight
of her eyes.

An uncle tips his high hat
and escorts her. Is it Sunday,
or a fop's way on the avenue
meeting skull with skull?

The merchant Fagus on her other side
considers, leaves his name
and message on a card:
"Collect my follies in a vase.
Just a bouquet from an admirer."

The uncle and the lady time their strides
and Fagus picks his way to comfort.

Little mood is to be gathered
from these sheepskin faces,
drumtight and wandering,
unless as primitive
I move my bulk no nearer
(brideless light affair)
but pass them with retentive eyes,
manifest and lonely.